DORLING KINDERSLEY *TRAVEL GUIDES*

KIDS'
NEW YORK

DORLING KINDERSLEY *TRAVEL GUIDES*

KIDS' NEW YORK

CHRISTOPHER MAYNARD

A Dorling Kindersley Book

DORLING KINDERSLEY
London • New York • Sydney • Delhi
Paris • Munich • Johannesburg

NEW YORK CITY

Senior Editor Giles Sparrow
Senior Art Editor Cheryl Telfer
Editor Kathleen Bada
Designer Darren Holt

Managing Editor Jayne Parsons
Managing Art Editor Gillian Shaw

DTP Designer Nomazwe Madonko
Picture Researcher Amanda Russell
Jacket Design Dean Price
Production Orla Creegan
US Editor Chuck Wills

First American edition, 2000
2 4 6 8 10 9 7 5 3 1

Published in the United States by
Dorling Kindersley Publishing, Inc.,
95 Madison Avenue,
New York, New York 10016
Copyright © 2000
Dorling Kindersley Limited, London

Library of Congress Cataloguing-in-Publication Data
Kids' New York.-- 1st American ed.
p. cm. -- (Dorling Kindersley travel guides)
Includes index.
Summary: A travel guide that focuses on the major sights of
New York and includes color photographs, listings, and
key facts.
ISBN 0-7894-5248-0
1. New York (N.Y.)--Guidebooks--Juvenile literature.
2. Children--Travel--New York (State)--New York--
Guidebooks--Juvenile literature. [1. New York (N.Y.)--
Guides.] I. Dorling Kindersley Publishing, Inc. II. Series.
F128.18.K46 2000
917.47'10443--dc21
99-053294

Color reproduction by Colourscan, Singapore
Printed and bound in Italy by Graphicom

For a complete catalog visit www.dk.com

Contents

STREET
PERFORMER

AQUARIUM FISH

FAO
SCHWARZ
CLOCK
TOWER

CONEY ISLAND
ROLLER COASTER

How to use this book

IN THIS BOOK YOU'LL find all
the information you need for a
wonderful trip to the Big Apple.
Each page features a popular sight
or attraction. Special color-coded
boxes list extra activities and
wacky facts about New York.

*The "Cool for Kids" box
contains suggestions for
other activities in the area.*

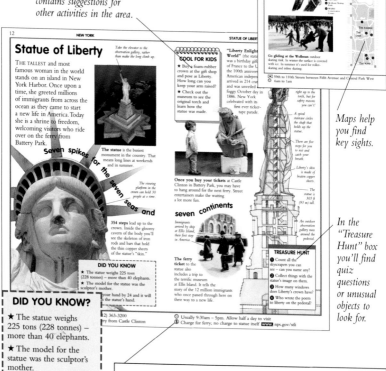

*Maps help
you find
key sights.*

*In the
"Treasure
Hunt" box
you'll find
quiz
questions
or unusual
objects to
look for.*

DID YOU KNOW?

★ The statue weighs
225 tons (228 tonnes) –
more than 40 elephants.

★ The model for the
statue was the sculptor's
mother.

★ Multiply your hand by
24 and it will be as large
as the statue's hand.

*The "Did You
Know" box pulls
out fascinating facts.*

SYMBOLS

The facts panel at the bottom of each page contains
essential details for each attraction. Symbols tell you
what type of information is being given.

✉ Address		⏰ Opening hours	
☎ Telephone number		$ Admission charges	
M How to get there		**www.** website address	

New York calendar

THERE'S ALWAYS A special event taking place somewhere in New York. Each occasion is a chance to celebrate the city's unique heritage. Fifth Avenue is the venue for many popular parades.

CHINESE DRAGON DANCERS

Every Fourth of July, the country celebrates the day it declared independence from Britain. New York Harbor is the best place to see spectacular fireworks.

FOURTH OF JULY FIREWORKS

Some balloons resemble well-known television characters.

Symbolic dragon dances and loud firecrackers mark the start of the **Chinese New Year** in January or February. If you want to join the festivities, head to Chinatown.

On Thanksgiving, in late November, American families get together to remember the early settlers' first harvest. New Yorkers celebrate with the **Macy's Thanksgiving Day Parade**, which has fantastic floats and gigantic balloons.

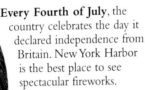

ANNUAL EVENTS

St. Patrick's Day Parade, March 17: traditional Irish festival.

Ninth Avenue International Food Festival, mid-May: feast of global food.

Puerto Rican Day Parade, first Sunday in June: traditional food and music on Fifth Avenue.

Halloween, October 31: the scariest night of the year.

Christmas tree-lighting ceremony, early December, Rockefeller Center.

New Year's Eve, Times Square: a ball slides down a pole at the new year's start.

Packed and ready

MOST KIDS THINK New York is great because it's so much like them – loud, noisy, and busy all the time. The only problem with visiting New York is that there's so much to see and do that it needs a bit of planning to decide where to begin each day. Some problem!

CAMERA

BINOCULARS

BACKPACK

Pack a backpack with all the things you need to explore New York. A camera is good for snapping sights you like. Binoculars are handy for getting the best view from the top of skyscrapers or during tours.

Buy a good map to plan where you want to go and to see where you've been. Take plenty of change for snacks, drinks, trinkets, and other useful stuff.

QUARTERS

Public pay-phones take 5, 10, and 25-cent coins. A quarter (25 cents) buys three minutes of talking time within greater New York.

Wear shoes that are comfortable for walking.

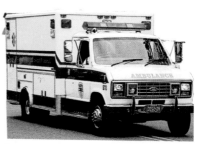

In an emergency, medical treatment is available at the big hospitals. If you have travel insurance, you may need to contact the company's emergency number as well.

Police, fire, and ambulance services ☎ 911
If you lose property in the street, contact the police.

Use tokens and **MetroCards** to pay for subways and buses. Kids under 44 in (112 cm) in height and traveling with an adult get to ride for free.

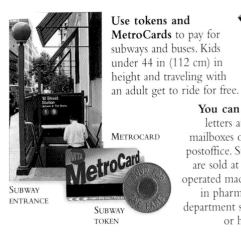

METROCARD

SUBWAY ENTRANCE

SUBWAY TOKEN

You can mail letters at blue mailboxes or at a post office. Stamps are sold at coin-operated machines in pharmacies, department stores, or hotels.

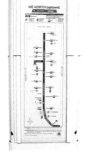

On buses you can pay with exact change as well as with tokens and MetroCards. If you need to switch buses, ask for a paper slip called a bus transfer.

DID YOU KNOW?

★ There are four main kinds of coin: 1 cent (penny), 5 cents (nickel), 10 cents (dime), and 25 cents (quarter).

★ There are six kinds of dollar bill: $1, $5, $10, $20, $50, and the rare $100. Bills are green and have portraits of former presidents on the front.

New York's police officers can be seen patroling in cars or walking the beat on the streets. If you get lost or separated from your parents, look for an officer, who will be able to help you find them.

POLICE OFFICER

Transit Authority Lost and Found ✉ 8th Avenue and 34th Street Station
New York Taxi Lost and Found ☎ (212) 221-8294

Getting around

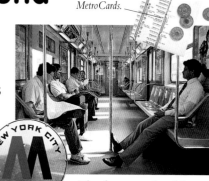

Fares are paid with tokens or MetroCards.

FINDING YOUR WAY in New York City is a piece of cake. Avenues run north to south, and streets run east to west. Low-numbered streets are downtown, and high numbers are uptown – and that's about it!

TRANSIT
AUTHORITY LOGO

The fastest and noisiest way around Manhattan is by subway. The trains clatter and roar, so it's great for yelling practice!

Get in through the front and out at the back.

Buses are a good way to watch the world go by, even if you do get stuck in traffic.

All New York cabs are yellow, and most seem to be battered. If the roof light is on, that means the cab is free – if it's off, it's taken. Whistling through your teeth and waving like crazy is the best way to hail one.

TREASURE HUNT

What color are:
1. Fire hydrants
2. City buses
3. Ambulances
4. Newspaper-selling machines
5. Standard mailboxes
6. Street signs?

The meeting clock also has train information.

Grand Central Terminal is very grand indeed. It's like a palace for railroads. It's also the fastest way north to the Bronx Zoo. The great four-faced clock is where people always meet – it's appeared in dozens of movies.

Information

🕐 Rush hours are 8 – 10am, 11:30am – 1:30pm, and 4:30 – 6:30pm

COOL FOR KIDS

★ Take a carriage ride in Central Park.

★ Go on a helicopter tour and look down for a change.

★ Take a guided tour on a double-decker tour bus.

★ Rent a bike to explore Central Park.

New York seems to enjoy bossing people around. Lampposts tell you where you are, which way to go, and when to cross, and may also have a load of instructions – mostly beginning with "No"!

East Side and West Side are separated by Fifth Avenue, which runs down the middle of Manhattan.

New Yorkers like to act rich and famous, even if they aren't. In fact, some people hire limos like taxis. You can't see in, but you can always try waving just in case it's a movie star.

Crossing the road in New York is simple – just wait for the sign to change from "Don't Walk" to "Walk," and then do it. Just be careful, and be sure the traffic has actually stopped before you cross!

That's when subways and buses get most packed and taxis are most scarce.

Statue of Liberty

Take the elevator to the observation gallery, rather than make the long climb up.

THE TALLEST and most famous woman in the world stands on an island in New York Harbor. Once upon a time, she greeted millions of immigrants from across the ocean as they came to start a new life in America. Today, she is a shrine to freedom, welcoming visitors who ride over on the ferry from Battery Park.

Seven spikes for the seven seas and

The statue is the busiest monument in the country. That means long lines on weekends and in the summer.

The viewing platform in the crown can hold 30 people at a time.

354 steps lead up to the crown. Inside the gloomy cavern of the body you'll see the skeleton of iron rods and bars that hold the thin copper sheets of the statue's "skin."

DID YOU KNOW

★ The statue weighs 225 tons (228 tonnes) – more than 40 elephants.

★ The model for the statue was the sculptor's mother.

★ Multiply your hand by 24 and it will be as large as the statue's hand.

✉ Liberty Island, New York Harbor ☎ (212) 363-3200
Ⓜ Subway 4 or 5 to Battery Park and then ferry from Castle Clinton

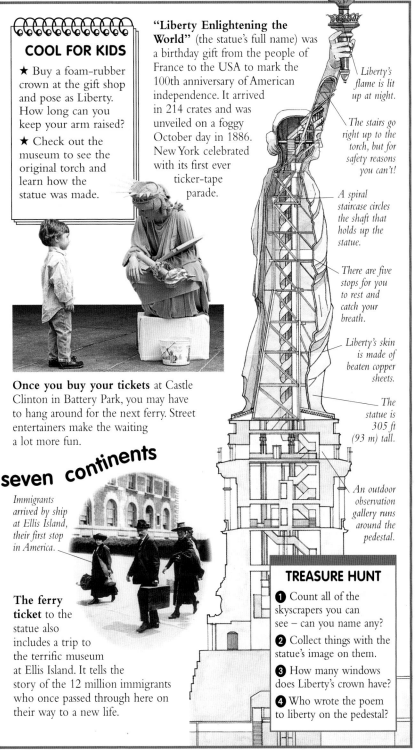

"Liberty Enlightening the World" (the statue's full name) was a birthday gift from the people of France to the USA to mark the 100th anniversary of American independence. It arrived in 214 crates and was unveiled on a foggy October day in 1886. New York celebrated with its first ever ticker-tape parade.

Liberty's flame is lit up at night.

The stairs go right up to the torch, but for safety reasons you can't!

A spiral staircase circles the shaft that holds up the statue.

There are five stops for you to rest and catch your breath.

Liberty's skin is made of beaten copper sheets.

The statue is 305 ft (93 m) tall.

Once you buy your tickets at Castle Clinton in Battery Park, you may have to hang around for the next ferry. Street entertainers make the waiting a lot more fun.

seven continents

Immigrants arrived by ship at Ellis Island, their first stop in America.

The ferry ticket to the statue also includes a trip to the terrific museum at Ellis Island. It tells the story of the 12 million immigrants who once passed through here on their way to a new life.

An outdoor observation gallery runs around the pedestal.

🕙 Usually 9:30am – 5pm. Allow half a day to visit
💲 Charge for ferry; no charge to statue itself **www.** nps.gov/stli

World Trade Center

IF NEW YORK WERE a forest, then the twin towers of the World Trade Center would be the biggest trees in town. The observation deck on top is probably the highest you will ever get without an airplane!

SPHERICAL SCULPTURE IN THE PLAZA'S FOUNTAIN

A great plaza at the base of the two towers is filled with modern sculptures. In summer you can listen to free concerts and see plays here.

Piggyback on the bronze animals.

SCULPTURE IN THE ROCKEFELLER PLAYGROUND

The Rockefeller Playground (Hudson River and Chambers Street) is one of the most popular play spaces in the city. Why? Because it has climbing nets, a carousel, a water-play area, and a garden of weird and wonderful sculptures.

COOL FOR KIDS

★ Look out for the penny flattening and engraving machine on the 107th floor of the World Trade Center.

★ You can stroll along the river path from Battery Park City to the very tip of Manhattan.

Two giant stainless steel towers loom over the baby buildings of **Battery Park City**. Once there were docks at this site. Now the area is full of offices and apartments. A walkway runs along the edge of the Hudson River.

✉ World Trade Center, between Church, Liberty, Vesey, and West Streets
☎ Observation deck (212) 323-2340 ☉ 9:30am – 9:30pm

After the towers, the walkway over West Street takes you to a cathedral of steel and glass called the **Winter Garden Greenhouse**. It's high enough for palm trees and has plenty of shops and restaurants, too. This is the way to Battery Park City and a bustling boat marina on the river.

Savor the view 1,350 ft (410 m) above Mother Earth. Even without the telescopes, you can see up to 55 miles (88 km) on a clear day. That's enough to notice the planet is curved.

Express elevators zip to observation decks on the 107th and 110th floors.

DID YOU KNOW?

★ The elevator gets you to the top in just 58 seconds.

★ The view is so popular that 80,000 visitors a day come for a look.

★ It can be clear at ground level, but cloudy at the top. If visibility is zero, don't bother to go up.

Ⓜ Subways to World Trade Center Ⓢ Charge
www. nyctourist.com/wtc

Wall Street

IF THE WORLD WERE LOGICAL, Wall Street would be called Money Street. Why? Because it's the home of banks, stock markets, and trading companies whose main business is making money. If your family owns any stocks or bonds, they may have come from Wall Street.

See the trading floor of the New York Stock Exchange from the visitors' gallery. It's the biggest stock market in the world, and it roars all day with the voices of brokers as they trade the shares of 3,000 companies. A short tour tells you how it all works.

A statue of George Washington stands outside the Federal Hall Memorial, which marks the place where he was sworn in as the first president on April 30, 1789. There's a museum inside, too.

Dollar, yen, mark, franc, pound, rouble,

Bank notes with a "B" were printed at this branch of the Fed.

COOL FOR KIDS

★ The nearest McDonalds to Wall Street (at 160 Broadway) has a doorman and a grand piano!

★ Buy ink and a quill pen at the Federal Hall Memorial Museum.

The Federal Reserve Bank (or the Fed) is the place where other banks bank. They come here to get freshly minted dollars and to hand back worn-out bills to be shredded. In the underground vaults is the largest store of gold in the world – 10,000 tons of the stuff. You need to be 16 years old to take the tour here.

NY Stock Exchange ✉ 20 Broad Street ☎ (212) 656-5168
Federal Reserve Bank ✉ 33 Liberty Street ☎ (212) 720-6130

DID YOU KNOW?

★ You can tell what job people do on the floor of the stock exchange by the color coat they wear.

★ Each gold bar in the Fed weighs 27 lbs (12 kg).

★ The vaults of the Fed are 5 stories down.

Way back when the Dutch governed New York (and called it New Amsterdam), Wall Street was the settlement's northern boundary. In 1653, a wooden wall went up to keep out the Native Americans and the British. By 1699, the wall was gone and only the name survived.

TREASURE HUNT

❶ Look out for the bronze statue of a bull. What's it doing here?

❷ The church here was once the tallest building in the city. What's it called?

❸ Which countries have the currencies listed below?

lire, peso, zloty

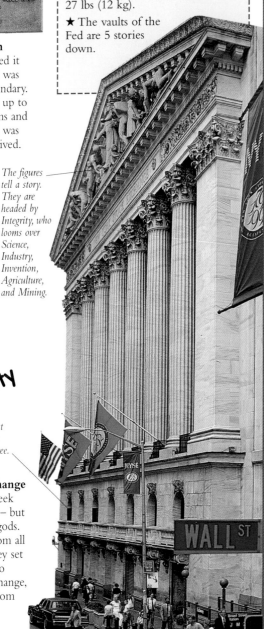

The figures tell a story. They are headed by Integrity, who looms over Science, Industry, Invention, Agriculture, and Mining.

The stock exchange first opened in 1792 under a nearby buttonwood tree.

The New York Stock Exchange looks a bit like an ancient Greek temple. It is a temple of sorts – but to money rather than to the gods. Inside, brokers trade stocks from all over the world. The prices they set here will cause waves in Tokyo tomorrow morning. The Exchange, which is around the corner from Wall Street, has been busy trading since 1792.

Ⓜ Broad Street or Wall Street ☺ Mon – Fri, normal office hours Ⓢ Free
www. nyse.com/public/educate; www.ny.frb.org

Children's Museum of the Arts

NO MARBLE HALLS HERE – just a wonderful arts playground that's the coziest place in the city to be creative. Do you like to mess with paints and plaster? Or dress up and perform on stage? This lively, touch-everything-you-see museum has it all.

TREASURE HUNT

❶ Find the graffiti wall and a piece of chalk, so you can add your own personal message.

❷ Look around for the ceiling that becomes a slide screen.

❸ Find the handmade mobiles that make music.

Wonderful things happen in the Artist's Studio every day. This is where you can mold castles of clay, sculpt paper bags, fold paper into origami shapes, and make things with sand and paint.

You can sow seeds that will grow into plants.

DID YOU KNOW?

★ The Ball Pond with its bold lily pads was inspired by French artist Claude Monet, who was famous for his paintings of water lilies.

★ The Playhouse has maps of the constellations drilled into its walls.

Make hand puppets of your favorite animals!

Turn into a star! Put on a costume to disguise yourself and pretend that you're somebody really famous. You can make costumes and sets in the theater space, and build some props, too. Then climb on stage and perform in front of your family and friends!

✉ 182 Lafayette Street ☎ (212) 274-0986
Ⓜ Subway 6 to Spring Street

WORKS OF
ART BY KIDS

The colorful entrance hall gives you a taste of what's to come. Grab a computer sketchpad to draw bright lines and weird shapes. Find the magnetic puzzle pieces and see if you can assemble a giant jigsaw puzzle that turns out to be a famous masterpiece of art.

Before creating your own art, look in the Children's Gallery to view work by kids from Japan, Australia, Venezuela, and other countries all over the world.

Work side-by-side with one of the museum's artists. They'll help you create original crafts to take home. If you're very lucky, one of your paintings may end up on the museum's walls.

A painted egg makes a wonderful present.

COOL FOR KIDS

★ The Art House is a two-story playhouse full of tools and building materials.

★ When they discover it's nearby, lots of kids get a burning desire to see the New York Fire Museum.

🕑 Thur – Sun, 12 – 5pm; Wed, 12 – 7pm Ⓢ Charge

South Street Seaport

LONG AGO, PEOPLE CAME to the city by horse or by boat. As a result, a necklace of docks once ringed Manhattan. The wharves are mostly gone now, but at South Street the old ships and cobbled streets give you a glimpse of the booming port that helped to make New York great.

The Seaport is seven blocks of old warehouses and streets, and takes in piers 15, 16, and 17. Pier 17 has shops, food stalls, and restaurants – and great views of the historic ships next door.

DID YOU KNOW?

★ The *Peking* is 347 ft (106 m) long and could carry 2,800 tons (2,844 tonnes) of cargo – about 15 blue whales' worth.

★ New York is still the busiest port in the country, but most of it is hidden in huge cargo terminals far across the harbor.

Six famous old ships are berthed here. The *Peking* is the second biggest sailing ship of its kind in the world. It has four tall masts – the tallest is 17 stories high. You can explore the ship or, on summer afternoons, listen to old sailors tell tall tales of the sea.

COOL FOR KIDS

★ Run away to sea aboard the old *Pioneer* schooner for a fun-filled harbor trip.

★ Lash yourself to a rocking mast in the Children's Center to experience a storm.

★ Visit the Seaport Museum for ship tours, workshops, and the story of the port.

All aboard to hear

✉ Water Street to the East River, between John Street and Peck Slip; Seaport Museum at Fulton Street ☎ (212) 748-8600 Ⓜ Fulton Street

At noon precisely, a black ball slides down the pole. Sailors once set their clocks by it.

A noisy carnival of street performers takes place at the Seaport. Acrobats, zany magicians, jugglers, musicians, and fire-eaters set out to entertain the crowd most afternoons.

This little lighthouse is a memorial to the many people who drowned when the *Titanic* hit an iceberg and went down in the Atlantic. It's by the entrance to the Seaport.

tall tales about the tall ships

🕐 10am – 6pm. Allow a half day at least 💲 Charge
www. southstseaport.org

Circle Manhattan

ISLANDS ARE PERFECT for visiting by boat, so a great way to see all of Manhattan Island is on a cruise. While you relax on the water, far from hot sidewalks and traffic fumes, one of the best views in the world glides past.

STATEN
ISLAND FERRY

For the best bargain in the world, take the Staten Island Ferry. It leaves Battery Park for an hour's round-trip ride across the harbor to Staten Island. You get the view, the Statue of Liberty, and plenty of sea air – and it doesn't cost a cent.

Admire the view from the bridge's walkway.

BROOKLYN BRIDGE

Sights at a glance

① *Intrepid* Sea/Air/Space Museum
② Chrysler Building
③ United Nations
④ Empire State Building
⑤ Chelsea Piers
⑥ World Trade Center
⑦ Battery Park
⑧ South Street Seaport

Most people island-hop by tunnel or bridge. The famous Brooklyn Bridge links the east side of Manhattan with Brooklyn. It was the first steel suspension bridge in the world.

Enjoy a thrilling ride at speeds of up to 50 mph (80 kph).

TREASURE HUNT

① How many bridges connect Manhattan to the mainland?
② What are the Palisades?
③ Can you spot the Little Red Lighthouse?

Circle Lines ✉ Pier 83, West 42nd Street ☎ (212) 563-3200; Seaport Liberty Cruise ✉ Pier 16, South Street Seaport ☎ (212) 630-8888;

COOL FOR KIDS

★ Subtract 40 from the number of a pier on the west side of Manhattan and you get the number of the closest cross street.

★ Visit Roosevelt Island Swiss-style by taking a cable car across the East River.

The United Nations (UN) headquarters is the one place in the world where nations can sit and talk to each other regularly. The UN does its best to solve squabbles between countries.

DID YOU KNOW?

★ A ship docks in New York City every 28 minutes.

★ The lighthouse under the George Washington Bridge was made famous by the children's story *The Little Red Lighthouse and the Great Gray Bridge*.

Bring binoculars and go skyscraper spotting. You can get great views of landmarks such as the 1930 Art Deco Chrysler Building. Its spire recalls the wonderful old radiator grilles that Chrysler once put onto its cars.

Williamsburg Bridge

Manhattan Bridge

MANHATTAN ISLAND

Brooklyn Bridge

Governor's Island

CHRYSLER BUILDING

Ellis Island

Liberty Island

There are loads of river cruises available. Choose an around-the-island tour or a short run that only covers the highlights. Tour guides are a goldmine of New York trivia.

Chinatown

IMAGINE A NEIGHBORHOOD that's part sardine can and part pressure cooker. That's Chinatown. It is so packed with wonderful sights, sounds, and smells that it feels as if you have been picked up and whisked away to Hong Kong. On top of it all, you'll never have seen as many restaurants in one place in your life!

The dragon is a Chinese symbol of good fortune.

New York Telephone

DID YOU KNOW?

★ The best time to see kite-flying is when the Chinese celebrate a festival.

★ Chinese have played dice games and games of chance since ancient times.

★ Many early Chinese immigrants came to build the great railroads that cross the country from coast to coast.

COLORED INK STICKS

PELLET DRUM

Public phone booths, mailboxes, street signs, and other familiar city furniture take on an Asian character in this part of the city. Even advertising signs have a Chinese flavor.

Chinatown is chock-full of stalls and shops selling cheap knick-knacks and cut-price designer brands (nearly all fakes). Stick to Chinese penny souvenirs – they are way better value if you want to buy trinkets.

✉ The dozen square blocks that form the heart of Chinatown are anchored by narrow streets like Mott, Bayard, Pell, and Mulberry

PEKING DUCK AND PANCAKES

A dab of plum sauce to smear on the pancake

Chinese restaurants serve a wide variety of food. Yummy, bite-size delicacies called dim sum are served up in dozens of tasty ways. For something really unusual, try **Dried Beef King** on Bayard Street. It sells a range of dried food, from sweet rice candy to curried beef.

Take a Chinese kite home with you!

More than 150,000 Chinese-speaking residents live, work, and play here. They give the place the feel of an exotic city within a city. You can hear people speak Asian languages and see Chinese character writing wherever you look.

At Chinese New Year – held on the first full moon after January 19th – the streets explode with the sounds of celebrating people and the deafening din of firecrackers. When Chinatown celebrates, bring earplugs!

Residents enjoy playing traditional Chinese board games.

TREASURE HUNT

❶ Buddhist temples welcome visitors to their peaceful shrines.

❷ Look for the bronze statue of Confucius at Confucius Plaza.

❸ Sample some of the best fruits, vegetables, and fresh seafood in the city at the markets on Canal Street.

The Empire State Building

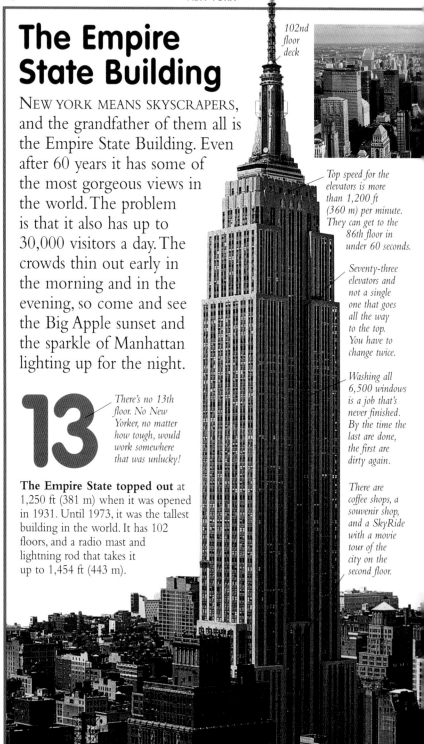

NEW YORK MEANS SKYSCRAPERS, and the grandfather of them all is the Empire State Building. Even after 60 years it has some of the most gorgeous views in the world. The problem is that it also has up to 30,000 visitors a day. The crowds thin out early in the morning and in the evening, so come and see the Big Apple sunset and the sparkle of Manhattan lighting up for the night.

102nd floor deck

Top speed for the elevators is more than 1,200 ft (360 m) per minute. They can get to the 86th floor in under 60 seconds.

Seventy-three elevators and not a single one that goes all the way to the top. You have to change twice.

Washing all 6,500 windows is a job that's never finished. By the time the last are done, the first are dirty again.

13

There's no 13th floor. No New Yorker, no matter how tough, would work somewhere that was unlucky!

The Empire State topped out at 1,250 ft (381 m) when it was opened in 1931. Until 1973, it was the tallest building in the world. It has 102 floors, and a radio mast and lightning rod that takes it up to 1,454 ft (443 m).

There are coffee shops, a souvenir shop, and a SkyRide with a movie tour of the city on the second floor.

✉ Fifth Avenue and 34th Street ☎ (212) 736-3100
Ⓜ 34th Street Station

VIEW LOOKING NORTH TOWARD THE BRONX

The two observation decks have spectacular views over the city. From the open terrace on the 86th floor you can see the boroughs of Staten Island, Queens, Brooklyn, and the Bronx. The 102nd floor is enclosed, but on a clear day you can see up to 80 miles (128 km) and take in five states.

There was no radio mast back in 1933 when King Kong climbed the Empire State Building.

HOLIDAY SEASON LIGHTS

The top 30 floors have banks of colored lights. Different combinations honor different holidays. In December the lights are red and green. On Valentine's Day they go red. For Independence Day they're red, white, and blue, of course.

No Hollywood star can rival "Old Stone Face" for its number of movie appearances (95 at the last count). Its most famous supporting role was in *King Kong*, when a giant ape climbed to the top to take on the Air Force.

An annual race to the top is held in February. The course covers the 1,575 steps from the lobby to the 86th floor. Male and female winners have each done it in under 12 minutes.

COOL FOR KIDS

★ Take a big-screen tour of the city in the New York SkyRide on the 2nd floor.

★ Bring along a handful of quarters for the big binoculars on the 86th floor.

🕓 9:30am – midnight (last elevator at 11:30pm). Allow at least two hours
Ⓢ Charge **www.** esbnyc.com

Chelsea Piers

THESE FOUR PIERS on the Hudson River were once the main passenger terminals for transatlantic ocean liners. Today they form an amazing 30-acre (12 ha) sports city. Think of a sport, and you'll be sure to find it here.

Protective clothing is a must.

You can roller-skate, inline skate, or skateboard at two outdoor roller rinks. There's also a skate school if you want to learn how to roll. Buy or rent your gear at the rink.

TREASURE HUNT

❶ Look for the four-story-high heated golf driving range, where you can rent kid-sized clubs.

❷ If it's sweltering outside, cool off in the Sky Rink, where there's ice all year round.

The Field House is a treasure chest packed with sports for children. Display your skills on the spacious basketball and volleyball courts, or pass the ball like a professional on indoor soccer fields lined with rich, green astroturf.

✉ Pier 62, 23rd Street on the Hudson River
☎ (212) 336-6500 Ⓜ Bus M23 to Hudson River

COOL FOR KIDS

★ At the baseball batting cages, automatic pitchers lob balls right at you.

★ A harbor tour by speedboat? Try the Chelsea Screamer.

★ Hungry? Try the Crab House's seafood or Rita's burgers.

For a taste of the Alps, try the huge climbing wall. It has routes graded from easy to ridiculously hard. If you're strong and nimble, you'll know where to go!

Get the hang of climbing – try a new view!

Think of Chelsea Piers as your sports-crazy fairy godmother. She offers year-round ice-skating and ice hockey, dance, karate, beach volleyball, golf, soccer, and 40 lanes of bowling.

With some practice you may be able to jump like this.

Inside the two giant gyms you'll find deep-foam diving pits, sunken trampolines, balance beams, pommel horses, and parallel bars – all the equipment a budding gymnast needs. Look for the toddler's gym with scaled-down equipment for the very young.

🕘 9am – 10pm 💲 Charge
www. chelseapiers.com

Intrepid Sea/Air/Space Museum

THE INTREPID FEELS more like a battle fleet than a museum. In one visit, you can explore an aircraft carrier, a destroyer, a submarine, and more – all floating on the Hudson River close to midtown Manhattan.

Learn about Intrepid's *role in* NASA's *space programs.*

During the 1960s, one of the carrier's jobs was to pick up astronauts after their space capsules splashed into the sea. On the hangar deck you can explore a space capsule or go online to see how the International Space Station is being created.

SPACE CAPSULE FROM THE GEMINI PROGRAM

Learn about the history of the carrier and its fleet on the hangar deck, where you can see an on-screen recreation of one of the *Intrepid's* wartime battles. Up on the bridge, you may get a chance to turn the ship's wheel.

The capsule has room for two astronauts.

COOL FOR KIDS

★ Sit in the seat of the gunners who protected the *Intrepid* from enemy planes.

★ Have a "dog tag" made up with your name on it – just like the ones US servicepeople wear.

These ships are not copies. The carrier *Intrepid* was built for World War II. It fought in the Pacific and was heavily damaged by attacks from kamikaze planes in 1944 and 1945. It served the US Navy for 30 years.

✉ Pier 86, West 46th Street and 12th Avenue ☎ (212) 245-0072
Ⓜ Subways toward 49th Street, then M50 bus west on 49th to the museum

The flight deck has planes from around the world.

The flight decks of the *Intrepid* are jammed with dozens of warplanes and some terrific hands-on exhibits. You can feel what it's like to drive a battle tank or to fly an F-18 fighter.

DID YOU KNOW?

★ The A-12 Blackbird gets so hot as it flies that it grows several inches in length.

★ Planes took off from the flight deck with the help of a steam-driven catapult.

★ *Intrepid* had a fleet of 105 planes.

The A-12 Blackbird could fly three times faster than a jumbo jet and twice as high. It was ideal for snapping pictures of the military secrets of other countries.

USS Intrepid

The USS Growler *was one of the Navy's first guided-missile submarines. It carried up to four missiles, all armed with nuclear warheads.*

The destroyer USS Edson

TREASURE HUNT

❶ Find the place where a kamikaze plane crashed into *Intrepid*'s deck.

❷ How many ships are there in the *Intrepid* fleet?

❸ Try to find the space thrill simulator.

❹ Where can you see the *Titanic*'s wreck on screen?

🕙 10am – 5pm, Tues – Sun in winter; all week long in summer
💲 Charge **www.** intrepid-museum.com

Rockefeller Center

THE CENTER IS A CITY within a city, containing 19 buildings and hundreds of shops. Lots of New Yorkers think it's best in December when a giant Christmas tree and decorations go up. The nearby Radio City Music Hall and the Museum of Television and Radio are fun to visit, too.

NBC LOGO

The heart of the center is the plaza. The Christmas tree-lighting ceremony held here every year attracts hundreds of spectators. In warm weather, the skating rink becomes a sunken café.

The tallest skyscraper at the center is the GE Building – home to the television network NBC. You can tour their studios and join the audience at the taping of one of their live shows.

The golden statue of the Greek god Prometheus watches over winter skaters.

COOL FOR KIDS

★ Go shopping in the Center's maze of underground stores.

★ Radio City is a national landmark. Even if you don't stay to see a show, you can take a tour of it any day of the week.

✉ Between Fifth and Seventh Avenues
Ⓜ Subways B, D, F, or Q to Rockefeller Center

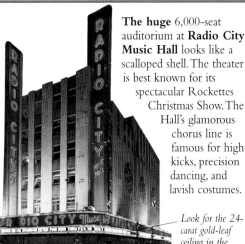

The huge 6,000-seat auditorium at **Radio City Music Hall** looks like a scalloped shell. The theater is best known for its spectacular Rockettes Christmas Show. The Hall's glamorous chorus line is famous for high-kicks, precision dancing, and lavish costumes.

Look for the 24-carat gold-leaf ceiling in the Hall's auditorium.

The Museum of Television and Radio has a collection of thousands of old programs. You watch screens in special booths or listen in radio rooms. On the weekend there are shows just for children.

TREASURE HUNT

❶ Track down the giant chandeliers at Radio City.

❷ Get leaflets for walking tours of the center inside the GE Building.

❸ Try the "Recreating Radio" workshop at the Museum of TV and Radio.

The public spaces of the center are full of statues, murals, and mosaics. The bronze statue of Atlas carrying the universe reminded people of Mussolini, the Italian fascist dictator, when it was first unveiled in 1937 – so much so that they took to the streets and protested!

Atlas is the ancient Greek god who was forced to carry the heavens on his shoulders.

DID YOU KNOW?

★ Radio City was built as the world's biggest and most luxurious movie theater.

★ The sloping Channel Gardens walkway gets its name from the way it separates La Maison Française and the British Empire Building.

American Museum of the Moving Image

THE TWENTIETH CENTURY is famous for creating moving images – things like movies, television, videotape, and computer games. Visitors to the American Museum of the Moving Image (AMMI) learn about each step of making, selling, and showing films.

RUDOLPH VALENTINO

GLORIA SWANSON

Many silent film stars made movies in Astoria. There are still working studios here.

DID YOU KNOW?

★ During a film, single images flow past your eye at 24 frames a second.

★ The AMMI contains costumes from the *Star Trek* television series and the *Star Wars* movies.

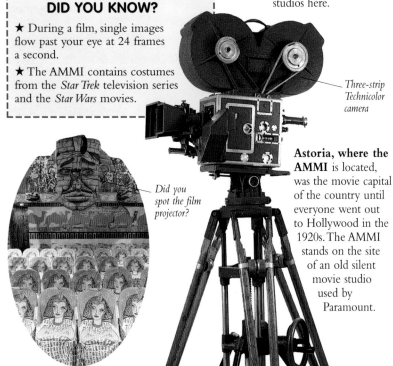

Three-strip Technicolor camera

Did you spot the film projector?

Astoria, where the AMMI is located, was the movie capital of the country until everyone went out to Hollywood in the 1920s. The AMMI stands on the site of an old silent movie studio used by Paramount.

Tut's Fever Movie Palace is a mock Egyptian movie house decorated in the style of the 1930s. It seats 35, and shows short films and old movies, such as *Zorro*.

✉ Corner of 35th Street, Astoria, Queens ☎ (718) 784-0077
Ⓜ Subway G or R to Steinway Street and a short walk

COOL FOR KIDS

★ Mix and match sound effects for *Terminator 2* and *Duck Soup*.

★ Create a slow-motion study of yourself on computer.

★ Dub your voice over Robert De Niro's image.

Behind The Screen is a two-floor, hands-on experience in creating movies. Learn how a story is made into a film through the work of screenwriters, a director, actors, and a large crew.

Robin Williams' bodysuit from Mrs. Doubtfire *is on display.*

Big-name stars bring a script to life.

ROBIN WILLIAMS AS MRS. DOUBTFIRE

The museum has thousands of objects used in making movies: cameras, costumes, props, and special effects. There is a free, hour-long guided tour at 2 pm every day.

BLUE-SCREEN EXHIBIT

You can try your hand at animating characters, playing with blue-screens, or messing around with sound effects.

DOLLS OF POPULAR TELEVISION CHARACTERS

TREASURE HUNT

❶ What's a zoetrope?

❷ Who was Marlene Dietrich?

❸ What did the television series *Charlie's Angels* have to do with school lunches?

❹ Can you find a boom?

The museum has zillions of still photos of actors, advertising posters, fan magazines, and other kinds of publicity material. You can see movie-related toys, dolls, lunch boxes, and soundtrack albums, too.

🕑 Tues – Fri, 12 – 5pm; Sat and Sun, 11am – 6pm 💲 Charge
WWW. ammi.org

Guggenheim Museum

HAVE YOU EVER HIKED inside a bicycle bell? Or moved through a high building without using elevators, escalators, or stairs? If not, you've missed one of the world's great wonders. The Guggenheim is more than a fantastic museum – it's a work of art in its own right.

CONSTANTIN BRANCUSI, *KING OF KINGS*

FRANZ MARC, *THE YELLOW COW*

Ordinary objects often appear in sculpture and artwork. They remind us that there's no limit to what people can use to create art.

The Guggenheim is full of interesting paintings. You'll have to use your imagination to figure out what the artists felt about the subjects they painted. Some paintings look like fairy tales, or the dreams you get after you eat too much. See if you can figure out each story.

When you enter the museum, take the elevator to the top. Then pretend you're a ball, and spiral downhill for a quarter of a mile as pictures, sculptures, and fantastic shapes go by.

There's a great collection of Impressionist paintings in the smaller side gallery.

COOL FOR KIDS

★ Daily tours are free for children, and on Sundays there are kid's tours and workshops.

★ Art deserves a treat. The basement café has space-age chairs and serves good food too.

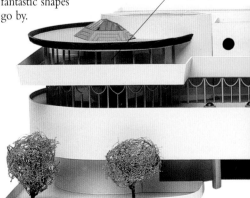

✉ 1071 Fifth Avenue at 89th Street ☎ (212) 423-3500
Ⓜ Subway to 86th Street

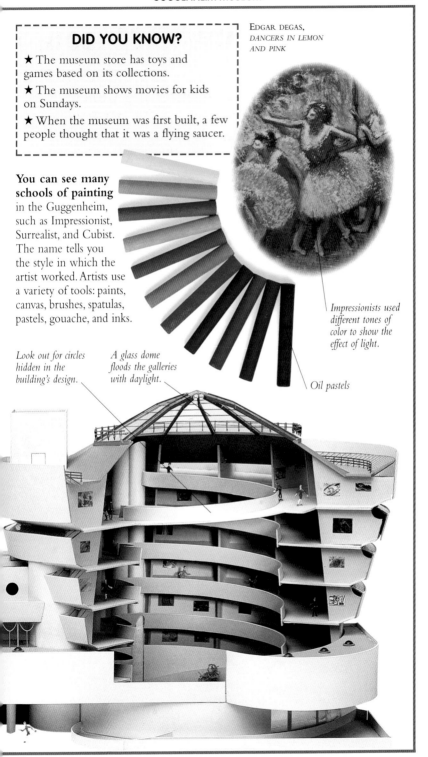

EDGAR DEGAS, *DANCERS IN LEMON AND PINK*

You can see many schools of painting in the Guggenheim, such as Impressionist, Surrealist, and Cubist. The name tells you the style in which the artist worked. Artists use a variety of tools: paints, canvas, brushes, spatulas, pastels, gouache, and inks.

Impressionists used different tones of color to show the effect of light.

Look out for circles hidden in the building's design.

A glass dome floods the galleries with daylight.

Oil pastels

☺ Sun – Wed, 9am – 6pm; Fri and Sat, 9am – 8pm; closed Thursdays
⑤ Charge for adults, free for children under 12 **www.** guggenheim.org

Central Park

FEW PEOPLE who live in Manhattan have gardens, so this is the back yard for an entire city. Some yard! You could spend days here and still miss half of it. Whether you want to picnic in a meadow, listen to storytelling, or visit great playgrounds, there's plenty to keep you busy.

At the boathouse on the Lake, you can rent rowboats and gondolas, or get bikes to peddle around the park. Tiny toy boats are also stored in the boathouse. See the radio-controlled boats race on Saturdays between March and November.

HAWK

Birds of all kinds can be found here. More than 250 species have been spotted in the park. Keep an eye open for birdhouses and beehives in the Ramble. You can find ducks at the Pond and turtles near Belvedere Castle.

Sights at a glance
1. Belvedere Castle
2. Loeb Boathouse
3. Hans Christian Andersen Statue
4. The Dairy
5. Wollman Skating Rink
6. Wildlife Conservation Center

CENTRAL PARK

THE RESERVOIR

THE RAMBLE

THE LAKE

THE POND

Go gliding at the Wollman outdoor skating rink. In winter the surface is covered with ice. In summer it's used for roller-skating and inline skating.

✉ 59th to 110th Streets between Fifth Avenue and Central Park West
🕐 6am – 1am

The zoo breeds endangered species, such as this red panda, to increase their numbers.

The statue of Hans Christian Andersen is a venue for storytelling on Saturday mornings.

There's a small zoo called the Wildlife Conservation Center. It has more than 100 animals from three different climate zones: the tropics, the poles, and the coast of California.

This storybook castle was modeled on castles found in Scotland.

Visit the Discovery Center at Belvedere Castle. You can borrow binoculars and guides to go bird-watching, or you can try out other nature activities.

BELVEDERE CASTLE

TREASURE HUNT

Try statue hunting – there are zillions! Look for:

❶ Beethoven
❷ Balto the Wonder Dog
❸ the Mad Hatter
❹ Shakespeare

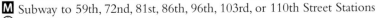

Ⓜ Subway to 59th, 72nd, 81st, 86th, 96th, 103rd, or 110th Street Stations
Ⓢ Free **www.** centralpark.org

Children's Museum of Manhattan

THERE ARE FIVE FLOORS of stuff to touch, look at, and play with at the Children's Museum of Manhattan (CMOM) – exactly what you need if you are a kid! Some exhibits are based on stories you may have read. Other exhibits help you learn about art, science, and television.

COOL FOR KIDS

★ In the Literacy Center there are books to read and storytellers to listen to every day.

★ The CMOM store has unusual souvenirs and clothing.

★ Create works of art in the Art Studio.

TREASURE HUNT

❶ Where can you ride the seven-hump wump?

❷ Try to track down the dog that writes poetry.

❸ Can you find dead skin cells?

❹ Where can you take part in a talk show?

The theater is the place to be for the best performances. You can learn dance moves, see puppet shows, or sing along with kids' choirs. A storyteller often drops by to tell exciting tales, and you're free to join in and have fun whenever you want.

CHUCK MANGIONE'S JAZZJAM

Learn how to operate a television camera and to edit video.

At the CMOM television studio on the second floor, there's a newsdesk, a weather map, cameras with special effects, and television screens for watching the show you made. The challenge is for groups to create their very own news programs.

Camera Operator 2

✉ 212 West 83rd Street between Broadway and Amsterdam Avenues
☎ (212) 721-1234 Ⓜ Subway 1 or 9 to 79th or 86th Street

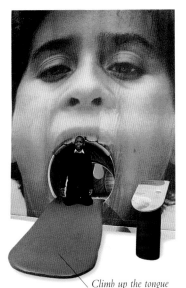

Take a Body Odyssey. Find out how the body works by journeying into a giant human figure. You can go through a blood vessel, down into the stomach, or even up into the lungs. See what happens to food when you eat, and to air when you breathe.

At the WaterWhirl you can learn about the power of water, and control its flow in a water maze. Use the water laboratory to experiment with water, and create floating artwork in the reflecting pool.

Climb up the tongue to enter Body Odyssey.

WATERWHIRL

DID YOU KNOW?

★ CMOM is one of only three museums just for kids in New York City.

★ Your body contains 50 trillion cells.

★ You can see the first drafts of Dr. Seuss's books at CMOM.

URBAN TREE HOUSE

The three-story Urban Tree House is outdoors, at the back of the museum. It's a play area that's a lesson in caring for the environment, too. It has displays and activities to remind us how to recycle and reuse ordinary objects every day. You can even try your hand at making compost with real live, wriggly earthworms!

A museum helper will show you the ropes.

American Museum of Natural History

IT'S THE BIGGEST museum in the world, says the *Guinness Book of Records*. After a visit, your feet are sure to agree! With more than 34 million exhibits on display, it would take you a lifetime to see all of them. What you need, then, is a smart plan or one of the museum's free guided tours.

This giant of a museum spans three city blocks. It houses a huge 3-D theater and a planetarium, as well as its famous exhibit halls.

TREASURE HUNT

❶ Search for Amazonian shrunken human heads.

❷ Track down the sea-going war canoe.

❸ Look for the 94 ft (29 m) long blue whale.

A mother *Barosaurus* rearing five stories high to protect her young greets you at the main door. In the **Dinosaur Halls** the show gets even better – watch as a robot dino head munches lunch, and don't miss the chance to touch and handle fossils.

Velociraptors *used their claws to slash prey.*

COOL FOR KIDS

★ Touch and explore everything in the Discovery Room.

★ Take a trip inside the human body in the Human Biology Hall.

★ The Dinersaurus Cafeteria is good – it even serves dinofries!

✉ Central Park West and 79th Street ☎ (212) 769-5200
Ⓜ Subway B or C to 81st Street

If the Earth could talk, it might say, "I suffer from indigestion – you call it earthquakes and volcanoes, I believe." The **Hall of Planet Earth** has all the gory details – and lots on weather and climate, too.

Go around the world in a day!

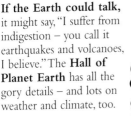

Azurite crystals

Goggle at $50 million in the **Hall of Minerals and Gems.** That's what the Star of India, the world's biggest blue sapphire, is said to be worth. There are loads of other valuable gemstones on display, too.

Go on your own African safari by wandering around the **Hall of African Mammals.** The stuffed animals in the ground floor dioramas look so real you almost expect to see them move.

This huge elephant herd greets you at the entrance to the Hall of African Mammals.

AFRICAN ELEPHANTS

Touch the Cape York meteorite – named after the spot where it crashed to Earth 10,000 years ago.

In the Meteorite Hall, you can see the rocks that astronauts picked up on the Moon's surface. Marvel at the Hall's biggest attraction – a 4.5-billion-year-old meteorite chunk that fell from outer space.

☺ Sun – Thurs, 10am – 5:45pm; Fri and Sat, 10am – 8:45pm
Ⓢ Charge **www.** amnh.org

Meet the neighbors

THINK OF A COUNTRY – from Afghanistan to Zimbabwe – and you're sure to see a little of it as you walk around. Most nations have informal embassies in the city in the shape of stores and restaurants. Turn a corner and you'll suddenly stroll into a neighborhood that's a world away from the USA. Neon signs and store names give clues to where everyone comes from.

Pickles served fresh from the barrel.

JEWISH PICKLE COMPANY

The Lower East Side has a big Jewish community that's been here since before World War I. Many shops are closed on Saturday, the Jewish Sabbath. That makes Sunday the best time to explore the bakeries and discount stores around Delancey and Grand Streets.

Latin American wooden sculpture from the Museo del Barrio.

Little Italy vibrates with excitement in September as the area around Mulberry Street celebrates the Feast of San Gennaro (patron saint of Naples, Italy). Streets are jammed, restaurants packed, and the stores sell pastry and ice cream to die for.

El Barrio, northeast of Central Park, is home to many of New York's Puerto Ricans. La Marquetta, the giant Park Avenue street market, sells tropical fruit, clothing, and wonderful carved figures. The nearby Museo del Barrio displays vivid Latin American art.

✉ Jewish Lower East Side between Delancey and Grand Streets; Little Italy around Mulberry Street

TREASURE HUNT

Feast your eyes! What kinds of food are:

1. lox
2. dim sum
3. helados
4. gyros
5. pretzels
6. falafel
7. heroes?

Little Korea is a fairly recent neighborhood of restaurants and stores crowding into 31st and 32nd Streets, not far from the Empire State Building.

Many Irish New Yorkers first settled on the West Side.

German New Yorkers have a niche at Yorkville.

Russian pockets are on the Lower and Upper East Sides.

Little India occupies East 6th Street.

DID YOU KNOW?

★ A green stripe is painted down the middle of Fifth Avenue for Ireland's St. Patrick's Day on March 17.

★ A giant dragon runs down Mott Street during Chinese New Year.

★ One of the best playgrounds in the city is in Carl Schurz Park by the East River in Yorkville.

Little Korea around 31st Street; El Barrio around 104th Street; Chinatown around Mott and Bayard Streets

Shopping

The Clock Tower is three stories high.

FIRST, THE GOOD NEWS. New York has some of the greatest shops in the world for children. Now, the bad news. If you could spend an entire year tracking them down, you would still not have enough time to visit them all.

The best toy store of all, say New Yorkers, is **FAO Schwarz**. Within its six stories is an entire zoo of stuffed animals. It's worth traveling miles just to see the famous musical clock by the entrance.

NIKE TOWN

Nike Town is a shrine to Nike sneakers that's also a theme park. You walk into a high-school gym, then discover it's a hall of fame. Apart from the amazing show, you can buy every kind of Nike shoe, too.

DID YOU KNOW?

★ Teddy bears take their name from President Teddy Roosevelt.

★ The annual Christmas Parade always ends up at Macy's department store.

★ FAO Schwarz started selling toys in New York in 1870.

Look for wands, scarves, and other magician props at Tannen's.

TREASURE HUNT

❶ Where do people go when they ride the huge robot at FAO Schwarz?

❷ How many of Carl Lewis's Olympic gold medals are at Nike Town?

The coolest magic shop in the world is **Tannen's Magic Studio**. It's the biggest, too, with more than 8,000 kinds of tricks. The sales staff will perform magic if you ask.

Bookshops for kids, such as Barnes and Noble Junior, are a great place to take a breather when your feet need a rest. You can browse and read for hours and, if you're lucky, you can listen to a passing author tell a tale.

STORYTELLING AT BARNES AND NOBLE JUNIOR

Take home some fun souvenirs from New York City. The choice is endless: from socks and sunglasses to tiny models of the most popular sights.

SOUVENIRS FROM
THE BIG APPLE

COOL FOR KIDS

★ My Favorite Place (267 West 87th Street) has a playroom, arts and crafts, and a great toy store – all in one.

★ Big City Kites (1210 Lexington Avenue) sells more than 150 kites, and loads more flying stuff.

Shop until you drop or you flop!

The Enchanted Forest of Toys is a toy store disguised as a storybook forest. It's filled with wonderful beasts, books, and great handmade toys. Look for the treehouse, waterfall, and bridge.

Studio ✉ 24 West 25th Street ☎ 929-4500; Enchanted Forest ✉ 85 Mercer Street ☎ 925-6677; Barnes and Noble ✉ throughout Manhattan

Bronx Zoo

JUST LIKE NOAH'S ARK, the Bronx Zoo has a couple of everything. There are more than 4,000 animals here, including some of the planet's most endangered species. The Bronx Zoo is one of the best zoos in the world. Its biggest enclosures feel as wild as safari game parks.

The Bengali Express monorail lets you goggle at wild animals from the safety of a track that's up in the air. Below you, deer and antelope roam. Elsewhere you might glimpse Asian elephants or the rare Siberian tiger.

Free-flying butterflies in the Butterfly Zone will flutter right up to you. It's open from May to October. Don't miss the giant caterpillar if you want to find out about the life of the monarch butterfly.

DID YOU KNOW?

★ The turtle shells in the Children's Zoo are big enough to wear.

★ The face painters will be happy to give you a real animal face on the weekend.

★ Get a bird's-eye view of the zoo from the Skyfari aerial tram.

★ Souvenir shops sell creepy-crawly keyrings, hibernation boxes, and soft toys.

COOL FOR KIDS

★ Go on a trek in the Baboon Reserve and discover the origins of gelada baboons.

★ Swap day for night in the World of Darkness as you watch nocturnal animals.

★ Meet the rare lowland gorillas in the Congo Gorilla Forest.

In the Children's Zoo you can become a beast. Prairie dog town lets you burrow like a prairie dog, then pop out among real ones. There's a heron's nest big enough to roost in, and a spiderweb of ropes to weave your way across.

Act like

📭 Bronx River Parkway at Fordham Road ☎ (718) 367-1010
Ⓜ Metro-North Railroad from Grand Central

BRONX ZOO

BRONX RIVER

HIMALAYAN HIGHLANDS

AFRICA

WILD ASIA

KEY
—— Skyfari
..... Monorail
- - - Shuttle route

Sights at a glance

World of Birds

Butterfly Zone

Children's Zoo

Elephants

World of Reptiles

World of Darkness

Camel Rides

Jungle World

Giraffe House

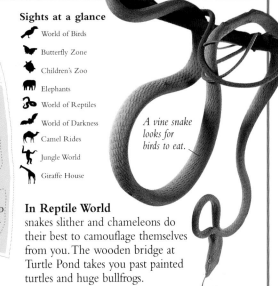

A vine snake looks for birds to eat.

In Reptile World

snakes slither and chameleons do their best to camouflage themselves from you. The wooden bridge at Turtle Pond takes you past painted turtles and huge bullfrogs.

Jungle World is an indoor tropical rain forest that is so real it even has five waterfalls. It's hot and humid in here and a great place to get close to a dozing gharial (a small kind of crocodile). You can also see tiny creatures close-up in the Unseen Multitude exhibition.

an animal in prairie dog town!

Real prairie dog

Human prairie dog in a see-through burrow!

🕐 Apr – Oct, Mon – Fri, 10am – 5pm; Sat and Sun, 10am – 5:30pm; Nov – Mar, 10am – 4:30pm 💲 Charge **www.** bronxzoo.com

New York Botanical Garden

THE BIGGEST WILD SPACE in all of New York is in the Bronx. Here you can roam and explore more than 250 acres (101 ha) of woodlands and wetlands, and even discover a lush tropical rain forest.

It's way too cold in New York for coconut palms to grow outdoors, but you can see them grow here inside a giant conservatory along with other tropical plants.

The most spectacular greenhouse in America has bananas, avocados, guavas, and cacti growing inside it. You can't pick the exotic fruit, but you can take a guided tour and see all of them.

Make compost and help harvest fruits and vegetables.

You can get very dirty when you dig, seed, weed, and water in the **Family Garden**. It's a real working garden – soil, worms, and all – where you can learn how to grow fruit, beans, and towers of sunflowers.

COOL FOR KIDS

★ Take a ride on the open-air tram.

★ Wander in the woodland trails of the 40-acre (16 ha) forest.

★ Go on a Plant Hunter's tour of the Conservatory.

★ Visit the Snap Dragon Snack Wagons.

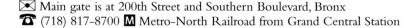

✉ Main gate is at 200th Street and Southern Boulevard, Bronx
☎ (718) 817-8700 Ⓜ Metro-North Railroad from Grand Central Station

For a bug's-eye view of plants and other insects, visit the nature lab at the **Adventure Garden** and get ready for a shock. With the help of the lab's powerful binoculars, you'll discover that the world is teeming with creatures that you never noticed before. You'll become a botanist in your own right!

Zoom in on insect life at the nature lab.

At the Adventure Garden you can walk across giant lily pads, explore a maze, and follow a wetland trail. You can even borrow a discovery cart with clues, crayons, and magnifying glasses to help you study the plants here.

Step inside the amazing world of plants!

Take apart a giant flower and try to put the pieces back together again.

TREASURE HUNT

❶ What do frogs eat for lunch at the Pond Café?

❷ Which fern's ancestors were food for dinosaurs?

❸ What is the name of the plant from which chocolate is made?

❹ Which plant is used as a musical instrument?

🕐 Tue – Sun; Nov – Mar, 10am – 4pm; Apr – Oct, 10am – 6pm
💲 Charge **www.** nybg.org

Coney Island

IT'S FAMOUS. IT'S FADED. And it's 100 percent tacky fun. This is New York's old-fashioned amusement park and the place to escape when you've had enough of museums and restaurants and good behavior in public. Here you'll get noise, excitement, and loads of junk food – guaranteed!

Kiddie areas in both parks have rides specially designed for kids – but if you're big enough, you can also go on the adult rides.

COOL FOR KIDS

★ The New York Aquarium is home to thousands of fish and sea mammals.

★ You can go crabbing off the Fishing Pier.

★ Try the beach. In hot weather it's the coolest place to be in New York City.

There are two parks by the boardwalk: Astroland and Denno's Wonder Wheel. The first has the legendary Cyclone, a 70-year-old wooden roller coaster. The second is famous for its giant 150 ft (46 m) high Ferris wheel. There are dozens of other rides, too, in both parks.

Even roller coasters are patriotic in New York!

THE CYCLONE

You can SCREAM as loud as

ASTRO

CYCL

✉ Surf Avenue, Coney Island, Brooklyn
Ⓜ Subways B, D, N, or F to Stilwell Avenue-Coney Island

A long subway ride across Brooklyn gets you to this famous playground by the sea. There's a boardwalk, two amusement parks, a beach, a pier, and the wonderful New York Aquarium just a few blocks away. A day at Coney Island is a chance for grown-ups to be kids – and kids to go bananas.

DID YOU KNOW?

★ The name of Coney Island is derived from the Dutch words Konijn Eiland, which mean "rabbit island."

★ At Astroland you pay one price for a ticket and get five hours to try all the rides.

★ A knish is a traditional Jewish snack. Try one at Mrs. Stahl's, 1001 Brighton Beach and Coney Island Avenues.

The Cyclone was born in 1927. It's an official New York landmark, up there with the Brooklyn Bridge and the Statue of Liberty.

Hot dogs don't get more original than at Nathan's Famous Frankfurters. Nathan's has been stuffing dogs into buns since 1916, when they cost a nickel (five cents) – it's $2 today! The wait in line here gives your stomach time to settle after all the rides.

Late May to early Sept, 12pm – 12am; April and Oct, weekends only

Charge **www.** astroland.com; www.wonderwheel.com

New York Aquarium

RIGHT BY THE SEA, just a short stroll from Coney Island, more than 10,000 fish, sea mammals, and sea birds live in the oldest aquarium in the country. Most of the exhibits are set up to look like natural habitats. You can learn about sea creatures and find out how they are protected in the wild.

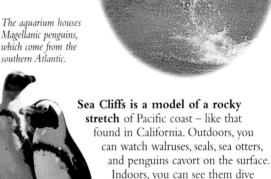

Try to stay dry when the dolphins perform!

Cheer, clap, and get splashed at the 1,600-seat **Aquatheater**. Every day from May to October, bottlenose dolphins and sea lions perform spectacular high-speed leaps and crash-landings that send water flying everywhere!

The aquarium houses Magellanic penguins, which come from the southern Atlantic.

Sea Cliffs is a model of a rocky stretch of Pacific coast – like that found in California. Outdoors, you can watch walruses, seals, sea otters, and penguins cavort on the surface. Indoors, you can see them dive into waves created by a special wave machine.

Beluga means "white" in Russian.

DID YOU KNOW?

★ The aquarium first opened in 1896. Today it covers a 14-acre (3 ha) site.

★ Bottlenose dolphins herd schools of fish in the same way cowhands herd cattle.

★ Knifefish use electricity to find their way in water.

The huge Whale Tank is home to a family of pure white beluga whales. This small Arctic whale squeals, clicks, and whistles so much that it is often called "the canary of the sea." The first whales ever to be born in captivity belong to the aquarium's beluga family.

✉ Surf Avenue and West Eighth Street ☎ (718) 265-3474
Ⓜ Subway D to West Eighth Street in Brooklyn

SAND TIGER SHARK

Stand under crashing waves (and stay dry) at the indoor **Discovery Cove**. You can touch horseshoe crabs, starfish, and urchins. There's a salt marsh to explore, exhibits about electric fish that go zap, and lots more to see and do.

THORNBACK RAY

At the Shark Tank you can watch big snaggle-toothed sand tigers glide past, and see sleepy nurse sharks doze on the bottom. The massive tank holds 90,000 gallons (409,000 liters) of water. Scientists study the sharks here to understand how they live.

QUEEN ANGELFISH

ROCK BEAUTY

"Dive" into tropical waters at the coral reef exhibits. The aquarium is home to hundreds of brightly colored, exotic fish. You can learn about the delicate environments in which they live.

Water everywhere – see the secrets of the sea

COOL FOR KIDS

★ Touch the rays at Discovery Cove – they enjoy being petted.

★ See an electric eel power flashing lights and create strange thumping sounds.

★ Find out how scientists study creatures underwater.

🕐 Mon – Fri, 10am – 4:30pm; Sat and Sun, 10am – 6pm
💲 Charge **www.** wcs.org/zoos/aquarium

New York Hall of Science

IT'S NOT DOWNTOWN, but who cares when it's the best. The New York Hall of Science is one of the top hands-on centers of science and technology in the US. The Hall has more than 185 amazing exhibits, and manages to turn science into a total blast.

Be a lab brat! At the second-biggest science playground in the world, you can slide, climb, and play as you learn about science. Teeter on the giant seesaw to show how levers work. Climb on a rope web to prove Newton's Third Law (for every action there is an equal and opposite reaction).

ROPE WEB IN THE SCIENCE PLAYGROUND

At Window on the Universe, you can link to astronomy websites all over the world via the Internet. A giant video wall of screens allows you to see images of space just like a real astronomer. In the **Technology Gallery**, you can play with the latest science titles on CD-ROM.

Staff are on hand to explain the Universe's mysteries.

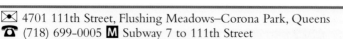

✉ 4701 111th Street, Flushing Meadows–Corona Park, Queens
☎ (718) 699-0005 Ⓜ Subway 7 to 111th Street

Turn into a giant and watch your parents shrink in the **Distortion Room**. This exhibit plays tricks on your eyesight to explain the way in which we see things.

DISTORTION ROOM

The microbes that live on a needle and thread are visible at this size.

Beyond the eye of a giant sewing needle you'll meet a huge collection of the tiniest creatures in the world. In **Hidden Kingdoms** you can magnify a drop of pond water until the microbes swarming in it are visible to the naked eye.

TREASURE HUNT

❶ Can you find the giant amoeba?

❷ Where is the machine that makes water flow uphill?

❸ Can you figure out how to work the remote-controlled telescope?

BUBBLE TABLE

Explore light and color with the 91 exhibits in **Seeing the Light**. You can blow giant soap bubbles, cast a colorful shadow, and see daily demonstrations of lasers.

🕐 Mon – Wed, 9:30am – 2pm; Thurs – Sun, 9:30am – 5pm
💲 Charge **www.** nyhallsci.org

Liberty Science Center

IN JERSEY CITY, just past the Statue of Liberty and Ellis Island, is a very cool and futuristic science center, with more than 250 hands-on, fun exhibits. To turn a visit into a great adventure, take the short ferry ride to the museum across the Hudson River.

LIBERTY SCIENCE CENTER

Each of the three floors at the center covers a different area of science. Look for the Hoberman Sphere – a giant expanding metal globe – at the building's entrance.

TREASURE HUNT

❶ Track down the wind experiment: How fast is the wind blowing today?

❷ Name the hottest parts of your body.

❸ Where can you take computers and photocopiers apart?

Down on the Invention Floor

VIRTUAL HOOPS

are famous creations for you to explore, such as a gramaphone – the first machine to play records. You can fly a jet-fighter simulator, play a virtual basketball game, or else go to the swap shop and pretend to be a real inventor.

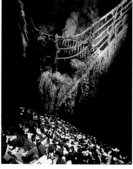

You'll sit glued to the biggest, most spectacular IMAX screen in the country in the **Dome Theater**. You can watch movies of sharks, wolves, ancient Egypt, and other amazing subjects.

Special glasses let you watch the screen in 3-D.

Light fever!

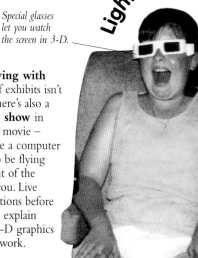

As if playing with dozens of exhibits isn't enough, there's also a **3-D laser show** in which the movie – born inside a computer – seems to be flying straight out of the screen at you. Live demonstrations before each show explain how the 3-D graphics and lasers work.

✉ Liberty State Park, 251 Phillip Street, Jersey City ☎ (201) 200-1000
🕐 Tues – Sun, 9:30am – 5:30pm 💲 Charge **WWW.** lsc.org

Explore the body and its senses on the **Health Floor**. Inside the pitch-black Touch Tunnel, you can learn all about your sense of touch. Try the quizzes on health and disease.

SKELETON PUZZLE

COOL FOR KIDS

★ Peer through a glass wall and look inside an active beehive.

★ Climb into a real ambulance and learn what happens in an emergency.

★ Try out the working crane and move stuff around.

MILLIPEDE

DID YOU KNOW?

★ The E-Quest exhibit has a geyser that spouts water 10 ft (3 m) high.

★ There are 4,000 different kinds of cockroach in the world, but only 100 are considered pests.

★ The Hoberman Sphere is made of aluminum and weighs 700 lb (318 kg).

On the Environment Floor there's a little estuary that's a mini version of the Hudson, a working solar telescope, and an insect zoo with residents you can touch! Climb the rock wall to discover what it takes to be a mountaineer.

Let the sights grab you at the great laser show!

M PATH subway to Exchange Place, then ferry from World Financial Center to Colgate Center, then bus to Liberty Science Center

Rainy days and indoor plays

EVEN NEW YORK CITY has bad weather sometimes. That's when places that are warm and dry, and where you can have loads of fun, are especially good news – such as theaters and indoor playgrounds. New York has lots of both.

Hackers, Hitters, and Hoops is fun for kids of all ages. This indoor sports park has everything from basketball courts and miniature golf to table tennis, along with an obstacle challenge.

They sing, they dance, they talk, and give a wonderful wooden performance!

You may get a chance to meet the performers before the show.

At venues like the Lenny Suib Puppet Theater, puppeteers come from all over the country to perform. You may also see magicians and clowns do an act. Shows last for about an hour.

People say the Paper Bag Players are the best kids' theater group in the country. Their props are mostly household stuff – cardboard boxes and paper bags. They do fast, funny shows and silly songs – you're free to join in.

When the weather's

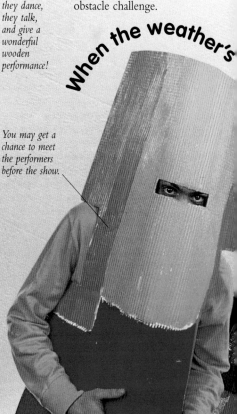

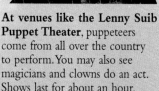

Lazer Park ✉ 163 West 46th St. ☎ (212) 398-3060; XS New York ✉ 1457 Broadway ☎ (212) 398-5467; Hackers ✉ 123 West 18th St.

When you play laser tag, you get handed a phaser to fire and a body vest that records hits. Then you creep into the foggy gloom of a huge maze to hunt for prey – other players! The biggest laser tag arena in Manhattan is **Lazer Park**.

LASER TAG

Headset has tiny television screen.

If you can handle the throbbing music and flashing lights, then electronic games arenas, such as **XS New York**, are as good it gets. Some of the virtual reality games – like the downhill skiing simulator – feel awfully close to the real thing! You'll enjoy these games best if you're 10 years or older.

The machine rocks to make the game feel real.

VIRTUAL REALITY MACHINE

wet, a show's a good bet!

Manhattan's oldest theater was built in 1900.

The New Victory Theater presents performances aimed at families and is open all year round. It puts on about a dozen original shows a year, with drama, puppetry, dance, music, and circus acts from all around the world. Best of all, its prices are incredibly low for a New York theater.

Lenny Suib Puppets ✉ 555 East 90th St. ☎ 369-8890; New Victory Theater ✉ 209 West 42nd St. ☎ 382-4020; Paper Bag Players ☎ 362-0431

Useful addresses

NEW YORK IS FULL of playgrounds and parks where you can have fun. If you get hungry, head to a nearby restaurant for a bite to eat.

PARKS AND PLAYGROUNDS

LOWER MANHATTAN

Robert F. Wagner Park
✉ Next to Battery Park City, southern tip of Manhattan

SEAPORT

Pearl Street Playground
✉ Fulton, Water, and Pearl Streets

SOHO AND TRIBECA

Pier 25 Children's Park
✉ North Moore Street and the Hudson River

GREENWICH VILLAGE

Washington Square Park
✉ Fifth Avenue between Waverly Place and West 4th Street

EAST VILLAGE

Tompkins Square Park
✉ Avenue A at East 9th Street

CHELSEA

Bryant Park
✉ Sixth Avenue from 40th to 42nd Streets

Madison Square
✉ Broadway from 23rd to 26th Streets

GRAMERCY

Union Square
✉ 16th Street and Broadway

UPPER WEST SIDE

Henry Neufield Playground
✉ West 76th Street and Riverside Drive

The "Hippo" Playground
✉ West 91st Street and Riverside Drive

The "Dino" Playground
✉ West 97th Street and Riverside Drive

77th Street Park (Wood Park)
✉ Amsterdam Avenue at 77th Street

CENTRAL PARK

West 67th Street (The Lauder Playground)
✉ Central Park at West 67th Street

Wild West Playground
✉ Central Park at West 93rd Street

UPPER EAST SIDE

John Jay Park
✉ 76th Street east of York Avenue

MORNINGSIDE HEIGHTS

Riverside State Park
✉ 145th Street and Riverside Drive

West 112th Street Playground
✉ 112th Street and Riverside Drive

The Dolphin Playground
✉ West 123rd Street and Riverside Drive

PLACES TO EAT

LOWER MANHATTAN

Gloria's
✉ 107 West Broadway at Reade Street ☎ (212) 766-0911

Odeon
✉ 145 West Broadway at Thomas Street ☎ (212) 233-0507

SOUTH STREET SEAPORT

Joe's Shanghai
✉ 9 Pell Street between Bowery and Mott Streets
☎ (212) 233-8888

CHELSEA

America
✉ 9 East 18th Street between Broadway and Fifth Avenue
☎ (212) 505-2110

Mary Ann's
✉ 116 Eighth Avenue at 21st Street ☎ (212) 633-0877

THEATER DISTRICT

Café Un Deux Trois
✉ 123 West 44th Street between Broadway and 6th Avenue
☎ (212) 354-4148

Carmine's
✉ 200 West 44th Street between Broadway and 8th Avenue
☎ (212) 221-3800

Ellen's Stardust Diner
✉ 1650 Broadway at 51st Street
☎ (212) 956-5151
✉ 1377 Sixth Avenue at 51st Street ☎ (212) 307-7575

Virgil's Real BBQ
✉ 152 West 44th Street between Broadway and 6th Avenue
☎ (212) 921-9494

UPPER MIDTOWN

Mangia
✉ 50 West 57th Street between 5th and 6th Avenues
☎ (212) 582-3061

UPPER WEST SIDE

Boulevard
✉ 2398 Broadway at 88th Street
☎ (212) 874-7400

Carmine's
✉ 2450 Broadway between 90th and 91st Streets
☎ (212) 362-2200

Good Enough to Eat
✉ 483 Amsterdam Avenue between 83rd and 84th Streets
☎ (212) 496-0163

Mary Ann's
✉ 2452 Broadway at 91st Street
☎ (212) 877-0132

CENTRAL PARK

Mickey Mantle's
✉ 42 Central Park South between 5th and 6th Avenues
☎ (212) 688-7777

UPPER EAST SIDE

Lexington Candy Shop
✉ 1226 Lexington Avenue at 83rd Street
☎ (212) 288-0057

Mary Ann's
✉ 1503 Second Avenue between 78th and 79th Streets
☎ (212) 249-6165

Index

Page numbers in **bold type** refer to main entries.

Acknowledgments

The author

Christopher Maynard first visited New York when he was 10 years old, and fell in love with its pretzels. He also remembers how hot it was. He continues to be a regular and enthusiastic visitor to the city. Christopher has lots of experience writing children's non-fiction. An author of popular and award-winning books, he has written for Dorling Kindersley and a large number of other children's publishers. His creative projects also include writing children's magazines, and producing exhibition posters and guides.

Dorling Kindersley would also like to thank the following people for their help in the production of this book: Maggie Crowley and Selina Wood for additional editorial assistance, Tory Gordon-Harris and Olivia Triggs for additional design assistance, Sue Lightfoot for the index, Chris Orr Associates for the map artwork on the inside front cover, Steve Gorton, Gary Ombler, and Malcolm Varon for additional photography, Josh Hetzler and Lisa Vargues for assistance in New York, and Marie Osborn for picture research assistance.

PICTURE CREDITS

The publishers would like to thank the following people for their kind permission to reproduce the following photographs:

Key: a = above; b = below; c = center; f = far; l = left; n = near; r = right; t = top

Every effort has been made to trace the copyright holders and we apologize for any unintentional omissions. We will be pleased to add appropriate acknowledgments to any subsequent edition of this publication.

Special photography:
Max Alexander, Geoff Brightling, Tim Daly, T. Foo, Colin Keates, Barnabas Kindersley, Dave King, Norman McGrath, Michael Moran, Tim Ridley, Karl Shone, Chris Stevens, Clive Streeter/Patrick McLeary, Paul Williams.

AKG London: Solomon R. Guggenheim Museum, New York, USA 36r. **American Museum of the Moving Image:** 34bl; Peter Aaron ESTO 35cl, 35cr, 35bl. **Ardea London Ltd:** Val Taylor 55tl. **Bridgeman Art Library, London/New York:** Solomon R. Guggenheim Museum, New York, USA 37tr. **British Film Institute:** 34tfr. **The J. Allan Cash Photolibrary:** 9tr, 9cl. **Chelsea Piers Management Inc:** 29tr, 29br; Fred George 29cr; Martha Cooper 28bl; Taku Taira 28tr. **Children's Museum of the Arts:** 18cl, 18br, 19tl, 19tc, 19tr, 19bl, 19tcr. **Children's Museum of Manhattan:** 41br; Ann Chwatsky 41tl, 41cr; Mark Avers 40b.

Corbis UK Ltd: Angela Hornak 15br; Jonathan Blair 43b; Michael S. Yamashita 38bl; Robert Holmes 8cr; Thomas A. Kelly 7cb; Yann Arthus-Bertrand 11tr. **The Enchanted Forest Toy Shop:** 47br. **Mary Evans Picture Library:** Library of Congress 12b. **Eye Ubiquitous:** Michael George 53tl. **The Solomon R. Guggenheim Foundation, New York:** *King of Kings,* early 1930s, Constantin Brancusi, © ADAGP, Paris and DACS, London 2000, (FN 561449), David Heald 36tl. **Robert Harding Picture Library:** 2c, 7cl, 9br; Alain Evrard 7tr. **Kobal Collection:** 27cl; Arthur George 35tr. **Museum of Television and Radio (New York):** Norman McGrath 33tr. NBC and the peacock logo are trademarks of the **National Broadcasting Company, Inc.:** 32tr. **New York Aquarium:** 71cl; Rick Miller 54cl; Tara Darling 55b. **New York Hall of Science:** 57tr; Robert Essel 56cl, 56br, 57bl, 57br. **Nike:** 46cl. **Quadrant Picture Library:** Alan Felix 8br. **Rex Features:** 42l. **Science Photo Library:** ESA/PLI 43tr. **Spectrum:** 10br. **Frank Spooner Pictures:** 23tr; Gamma/Vogel Liason 52cr. **Turner Ent.:** 27c. **Malcolm Varon Photography:** 33br. **Wildlife Conservation Society, Central Park Zoo:** 39tr.

The street signs on page 11 are used with the permission of the New York State Department of Motor Vehicles.

The subway logo on page 10 is used with the permission of the New York City Transit Authority.

Personal details

A DIARY IS A GREAT WAY to capture
memories of a wonderful visit to the
Big Apple. Start your personal record here.

My Name ....

My Age ....

My Home Address ....

....

....

....

Arrival

I arrived in New York on ....

at ....

The journey was ....

Hotel

I stayed at ....

My room number was ....

My visit lasted ....

Departure

I left New York on ....

at ....

The journey was ....

I visited New York with ....

....

....

New York favorites

USE THESE PAGES to record your favorite
experiences from your trip to New York.

What were the best
places you went to?

....
....
....
....
....
....

What was the single best thing that you
did in New York?

....
....
....

What was the tallest building you
went up in New York?

....
....
....
....

What could you see from
the top?

....
....
....
....
....

What was the best souvenir you collected on your trip?
Where did you buy it?

....
....
....

New York has a huge
variety of foods
available – list the
different things
you tried, and
whether you
liked them
or not!

Plenty of food for thought!

....
....
....
....
....
....
....

What was the best trip you took while in New York?

....
....
....

Stick your favorite New York photo here!

I-spy

WHEN YOU'RE OUT and about in New York,
you can try these fun activities with your family.

Who will be the first to spot these New York sights?

Statue of Liberty

Subway station entrance

Police officer

Yellow cab

Empire State Building

Hot dog vendor

Billboard for a Broadway show

10/14/98   3H ADULT
CIRCLE LINE CRUISES
FAVORITE BOAT RIDE
EE HR SAILING

I ♥ NY

Collect these **souvenirs** and
keep them in the pocket at
the back of this book:

❶ Subway map
❷ MetroCard
❸ Postage stamp
❹ One-dollar bill

❺ Pencil from a museum
❻ Flyer for a Broadway show
❼ Subway token
❽ Empire State Building ticket
❾ Badge of a popular sports team
❿ Postcard of a famous sight

Funtastic New York facts

HERE ARE some interesting facts about New York that you might not know!

★ Central Park is five times as long as it is wide.

★ Macy's is the world's largest store, with 2.1 million sq ft (1,950,000 sq m) of floor space.

★ New York was named after James, Duke of York, the brother of King Charles II of England.

★ The New York Marathon is one of the world's largest city marathons, with more than 32,000 runners.

★ The Empire State Building has a mooring mast for airships.

★ The Unisphere is the symbol of the 1964 World's Fair.

CITY STATS

Area: 301 sq miles (779 sq km)
Population: 7,420,100
Boroughs: Bronx, Brooklyn, Manhattan, Queens, Staten Island

★ St. John the Divine is the world's largest Gothic cathedral. After more than 100 years of construction, it's still incomplete!

★ Taxi cabs are yellow because the founder of the first cab company believed that yellow was easy to spot.

★ New York has a nickname – Gotham!

★ The Metropolitan Opera is the world's largest opera house. It seats 4,065 people.

UNISPHERE IN QUEENS

New York quick quiz

BY THE END of your trip, you'll be a New York expert. How many questions can you answer?

1 In which building do representatives of the world's nations meet?

....

2 Which building is the tallest skyscraper in New York?

....
....

3 A US Air Force bomber crashed into which building?

....
....

4 Which museum features a spiral walkway?

....

5 In what part of Manhattan can you find telephone boxes with pagoda-style roofs?

....

6 Where can you visit a castle? ....
....

7 What type of metal is the Statue of Liberty made from?

....
....

8 Where can you see dinosaur eggs? ....

9 How wide is the largest IMAX screen in the USA?

10 Where can you see images taken by telescopes in space?

11 Which local community celebrates the Feast of San Gennaro?

Who made the hot dog famous?

12 Where do the bull and the bear meet? ....

13 Which pier was meant to be the docking point for the *Titanic*?

14 Where can you find a giant musical clock?

15 Where can you see snow leopards?

16 Who performs with props made of cardboard?

17 What is the name of the world's second-largest tall ship? ....

18 Which museum saw action in World War II?

19 Where can you see otters, sea lions, and walruses? ....

20 Where can you see paintings by children from around the world?

Answers

TREASURE HUNT

Page 10
1. Red.
2. Blue and white.
3. White and orange.
4. Green.
5. Blue.
6. Green and white.

Page 13
3. Twenty-five. 4. Emma Lazarus.

Page 17
1. Near the Customs House; it symbolizes Wall Street.
2. Trinity Church.
3. USA & Canada, Japan, Germany, France, Britain, Italy, Russia, Mexico, Poland.

Page 18
2. The Art House. 3. The Actor's Studio.

Page 21
1. Steel.
2. 1,513 people.
3. With cobblestones.
4. Port, left side; starboard, right side.

Page 22
1. Sixteen.
2. Spectacular cliffs along the Hudson River, across from Upper Manhattan.
3. Under the George Washington Bridge.

Page 31
2. Five, including the *Intrepid*.
3. On the hangar deck.
4. USS *Growler.*

Page 35
1. Early device used to view animated characters.
2. Glamorous movie star of the 1930s and the 1940s.

3. The show's three stars appeared on many lunch boxes.
4. Behind the Screen exhibit.

Page 40
1. SEUSS!
2. MAX (A Dog).
3. Body Odyssey.
4. Time Warner Media Center.

Page 42
1. The Hall of South American Peoples.
2. The Hall of Northwest Coast Indians.
3. The Hall of Ocean Life.

Page 45
1. Russian Jewish smoked salmon.
2. Chinese small snacks.
3. Shaved ice with syrup poured on the top.
4. Warm pita bread filled with meat, salad, and sauce.
5. Salty baked dough in a knot shape.
6. Deep-fried ball of ground chickpeas made zingy with onion, peppers, and other spices.
7. Long French loaf sandwich.

Page 46
1. The first floor.
2. Eight.

Page 51
1. Flies, small beetles, slugs, worms.
2. The elephant fern.
3. Cacao.
4. Bamboo.

Page 57
1. Hidden Kingdoms.
2. Archimedes screw in the Science Playground.
3. Window on the Universe.

Page 58
1. The Weather Station.
2. The Thermography display.
3. The Swap Shop.

QUICK QUIZ

❶ The United Nations Building.
❷ World Trade Center, Tower A, 1,368 ft (417 m).
❸ The Empire State Building.
❹ The Guggenheim.
❺ Chinatown.
❻ Belvedere Castle in Central Park.
❼ Copper.
❽ The American Museum of Natural History.
❾ 88 ft (27 m) wide – the screen at the Liberty Science Center.

❿ Window on the Universe at the New York Hall of Science.
⓫ The Italian-American community.
⓬ At the New York Stock Exchange.
⓭ Pier 59 at Chelsea Piers.
⓮ At FAO Schwarz.
⓯ The Bronx Zoo.
⓰ The Paper Bag Players.
⓱ The *Peking.*
⓲ *Intrepid* Sea/Air/Space Museum.
⓳ The New York Aquarium.
⓴ The Children's Museum of the Arts. Nathan's Famous Frankfurters on Coney Island, Brooklyn made the hot dog popular.